.

SEED AND SOIL

SEED AND SOIL

Evangelist Mark Dunfee

Dedication

I want to dedicate this book to the pure in heart. The Kingdom of God, LIKE A MIGHTY ARMY, marches forward because of you. And if your heart has grown cold, been broken, or become bitter, it's not too late.

Even if you have given up all hope, you too can have a perfect heart given to you by Jesus. That's why Jesus had me write this little book for you.

Contents

Introduction

In my early days as a pastor, I preached in a little town and poured my heart out as I preached the Word of God. A young man in his late teens would sit down at the front, to my left, and was quite obviously less than thrilled with being in God's house. My preaching never moved him, and God's Word, as far as I could see, ran off him like *water off a duck's back.*

Years later in field ministry, I saw him in another state in a church where I was preaching. The handsome young man stood on the platform playing a bass and worshipping God to the point of tears. He was sold out to God and zealously following Jesus with all of his heart.

Though I am not a proponent of missionary

dating, I can tell you that Jesus and the little blonde pastor's daughter that he married changed his heart.

Priorities in life and what we believe all come from the heart. Kings in the Old Testament sat on the same throne, but God judged them according to their heart. Many a king had the character obituary that he followed God but not with a perfect heart.

Yet the kings that God specially blessed walked before the God of Heaven and Earth with a perfect heart. David, the shepherd boy who became king, was the one God found when He sought for a man after His own heart (1 Samuel 13:14)

God is still searching today. The eyes of the Lord still look throughout the Earth, searching the hearts of men and women, looking for a perfect heart that He can *bless and use mightily.*

> "For the eyes of the LORD run to and fro throughout the whole earth, to shew himself strong in the behalf of them whose heart is perfect toward him." (2 Chronicles 16:9)

God will look at your heart sooner than He looks at anything else. The moment Jesus comes into your heart, He will begin to sanctify it. Sanctification is a work in the heart that manifests in the life that is lived.

The soil of a perfect heart is a life that God can use without limits. Ask the Holy Spirit to create that kind of heart in you. *You can change the whole world when God changes your heart.*

Oh, how God loved King David and how King David loved God. God uses people that are not perfect, and the *blood of Jesus* makes them the *righteousness of God in Christ Jesus.* David's perfect heart always led him in the end to worship and do what was right.

King David is the first man mentioned in the New Testament. He is also the last man mentioned in the New Testament. For all of eternity, Jesus will literally sit upon the THRONE OF DAVID.

For some reason Jesus loves to be associated with those that the world and even the church have given up on. The love of God will never ever give up on you, *no matter what you have said or done.*

Some of you have longed for greater fruitfulness and longed for God to raise you up to do something that will matter for all of time and eternity. But ability and talent are not enough.

They never are. *Being used of God is a matter of the heart.*

There is a *loving hand* that will never leave you like He found you. God's great mercy saved me from a selfish life. Believe me that if Jesus can use me, He can use anyone. If you will only give Him access to your heart.

Let God put within you a perfect heart. It is the soil where the sower will sow God's Word. When you receive this revelation of Seed and Soil that Jesus taught, your whole life and your family's lives will never be the same. Forever.

Your friend,

Evangelist Mark Dunfee

1

The Parable of All Parables

"Then Jesus said to them, 'If you can't understand the meaning of this parable, how will
you understand all the other parables?'"
(Mark 4:13 NLT)

The crowd was so large by the lake shore that Jesus was nearly pressed into the water. They kept coming and coming from all directions. It was then that the Lord got into a boat and pushed back from the shore.

The water and shoreline formed a natural amphitheater to be easily heard. So, in a boat in front of a huge crowd, the Master Teacher taught the Parable of all Parables. He taught on SEED AND SOIL.

Jesus said to the masses, "If you do not understand this story, how can you understand any other story that I teach you?" The Lord was a storyteller. He taught the great spiritual truths with stories.

The *truth* that was taught by the Sea of Galilee there that day will also change your life today. It will change your family's lives forever.

It will take care of your past and never ever let you be a prisoner of it again.

This teaching of Jesus will supernaturally *bless* your future. It will cause you to be blessed now and look forward to even greater blessings in the future. Seed and soil will change your life forever. It will bring financial healing for eternity.

Seed and Soil

Seed with no soil can accomplish nothing. It cannot bring increase and the seed cannot multiply. Yet soil with no seed produces no harvest. The soil with no seed yields no fruit. No golden grain. No vegetables or crop to be harvested.

All the seed on the planet cannot amount to

anything without soil. Yet the most glorious field must have someone walk upon it to plow it and plant the precious seed. *Soil must have the seed and seed must have the soil.*

In Mark chapter four, Jesus was teaching a foundational truth of the Kingdom (seed and soil). One cannot produce without the other. *The yield and increase of the seed are determined by the quality of the soil.*

It is vital to give and to give in the right place. Financial healing is ready to come into your family when you decide to become a giver.

Have you ever heard someone say, "I give but I never seem to get blessed"? Of course, their confession is wrong, but a person like this may also be giving in the wrong place. They also may be in a church of unbelief.

Farmers are constantly examining both their

seed and their soil. These two elements work together to produce the harvest. It works that way in the natural world and it works that way in the spiritual world. In fact, the natural world is a reflection of the real world of the spirit.

The Soil Affects the Harvest

"Other seed fell on shallow soil with underlying rock. The seed sprouted quickly because the soil was shallow." (Mark 4:5 NLT)

Jesus taught about seed that fell in different types of soil. Mark 4:7 tells of seed that fell among thorns. But Mark 4:8 tells the wonderful news of seed being planted on fertile, good ground.

Note: The seed was all the same but the soil was different. The difference in the soil affected the harvest.

Jesus taught that the seed is the message of Christ's Kingdom. The soil is a way of describing people's hearts. How often I have seen precious men of God plow, and pick rocks, and sow the seed of God's Word among the hard-hearted. Sometimes people's heads are hard because their hearts are hard.

God may give you a tough assignment or Jesus may call you to a tough place. That is not what I am talking about. But young man or young woman, why spend your precious life among people that have heard the Good News about Jesus for generations and perpetually reject the message?

I have seen men that, because they would

never step out of their comfort zone, limited how much God could use them. Don't ever get bitter over a cold, backslidden group of people that are stony ground.

Love them and forgive them, and never throw away your seed. If you are called to preach, never ever let the devil tell you that you "don't have it" and that you and your spouse aren't good enough to preach the Gospel.

I'm saying this in great love, but do not waste your life on people that do not really want help and then try to make you think that their problems are your fault.

The Pharisees and the Sadducees will make your life hard and steal most all of your dreams and joy if you let them. That's what rocky and hard, unbroken, and unplowed ground does to good seed.

God may train you in a place like that, but when they constantly reject you, they have rejected the One who sent you. All that you have to do is forgive and to put things in perspective.

Often the reason that someone has a failure or setback is not because of the Word that was preached or the life that was lived. It was because of the cold, hard, rocky, sandy, and worthless soil within.

Repentance always can and always will change all of that. But repentance is a choice and people that have a religious spirit have made a series of wrong choices.

Often churches do not really want a pastor but desire a hireling to work for them and to do as they are told. So many times, I have diligently tried to plant where the ground was hard and the soil had very little life in it. Then the Lord Jesus sent me to lush, fertile soil and it changed our lives and ministry forever.

Sometimes that new soil didn't look like much in the natural, and it took a lot of faith to begin again. But once I started plowing, I never looked back. *You will never build a great life or ministry or marriage by looking backwards.*

Seek a Pure Heart

When you ask Jesus for a husband or a wife, take time to look beyond the outer appearance and look at their heart. Living a lifetime with a hard-hearted and angry man or a bitter and mean-hearted wife is pretty tough. God can change anyone, but they have to want to change.

When you marry a project with a hard heart,

you have signed up for tiresome toil and countless hassles. Don't let it happen to you, but keep a pure heart and then let the Holy Spirit send someone into your life that bears witness with your Godly spirit deep within.

Pastor, you can save yourself and your church so much grief if when you hire staff, you hire them for attitude and not just ability. *It is a whole lot easier to increase some people's skill-set than to change some people's attitude.*

Every business person needs to make God their partner and let the Holy Spirit lead them to people that they can do business and work with that have a good spirit. Extra prayer and a lot less rushed, under pressure, quick decisions can save anyone from so much trouble.

Walking in Holy Ghost discernment and taking some wise counsel from people with a proven track record will bring a whole lot of forever blessing your way. It will bring so much blessing of every kind your way that you'll be able to share it with others.

"Where no counsel is, the people fall: but in
the multitude of counsellors there is safety."
(Proverbs 11:14)

The Word doesn't affect everyone the same way. That is the teaching of the seed and the soil. Two people go to church and both hear the very same message and sit under the same anointing. One leaves God's house forever changed while the other person was bored and unchanged.

The message was the same, but the hearts of the two individuals were completely and totally different. Sin and pride, which often lead to bitterness, will spiritually harden your heart and take you away from the love walk that God designed for His children.

2

The Hard Soil of a Hard Heart

Dear friend, your heart matters to God much more than your talent and looks and all of your abilities combined. Talented people are everywhere. People with pure hearts are not.

The soil of your heart determines what the seed of God's Word can produce. Are you hard-hearted? Has a root of bitterness sprung up in the soil of your heart?

> "And I will give you a new heart, and I will put a new spirit in you. I will take out your stony, stubborn heart and give you a tender, responsive heart." (Ezekiel 36:26 NLT)

Let the Holy Spirit touch and remove anything and everything that should not be in your heart today. Forgive everyone that has ever hurt you and your family and come against you.

The more that God wants to use you, the more He will plow deep furrows in the soil of your heart and weed out anything and everything that is not of Him. But God plows in great love, and anything that He takes out, *He replaces with something that is so much better.*

Check Your Heart's Soil

Recently God began to deal with me about something wonderful that He wanted to bring into my life. Major expansion and fruitfulness, and *supernatural blessing* on a scale like nothing that we had ever seen before. Bigger and better than anything that I had ever received before.

I immediately began to disqualify myself by thinking that it was too big. That I didn't deserve it. That I couldn't afford it. What God has called me to do is way bigger than anything that I can achieve in the natural. *But God can achieve it through my life as I yield my all to Him.*

What I can't do, my God can. I've asked Jesus to use me in such a way that people I know will say, "He never could have done that by himself," so God gets *all of the glory.*

Whenever you sense that you are not responding to the Word like you should, always check the soil of your heart. It is so important to check the soil of one's heart, especially to see if your love walk is where it should be.

Love doesn't hate, isn't jealous, and doesn't hold grudges. It isn't bitter over some real or imagined slight or hurt feelings. Love forgives and acts like it never even happened at all (1 Corinthians 13).

God Is Seeking a Heart to Bless

The Word always works, every time. If something ever is not working right in your life, never blame God. *It is never the Word that is wrong or not working.*

Seed that is sown on cement or hardtop will not produce much of a harvest. The seed of God's Word is always seeking the soil of a humble heart to multiply and bless eternally. The problem is always on the human end of flesh and bone.

Think of the people who actually heard the Apostle Paul teach the Pauline Revelation of grace and faith, yet their hearts were so hard that they could not receive salvation.

There were even those who sat in the fields by the Sea of Galilee, but the Sermon on the Mount and the teaching of the Beatitudes never reached them. Even the actual words of Jesus which they actually listened to in person did not penetrate their cold, dead heart.

The heart of man is not good and is sinful until it has been born again. Have you ever asked Christ into your heart? Pray aloud this simple prayer, in faith, believing:

Heavenly Father, in Jesus' name, please forgive me for all of my sin. I believe that You are the true Son of God, and I claim Your shed blood on the cross of Calvary to pay for my sins. I believe that God raised Jesus from the dead. Wash me clean from all of my sins, and I will serve You the rest of my life. One day, I want to go to Heaven and live with You forever.

Our loving God, who is so rich in mercy, will forgive you now and wash your sins away. As a boy in church, we sang out of the hymnal, "I came to Jesus, weary, worn and sad. He took my sins away. He took my sins away. And now on Him I throw my every care. He took my sins away."

Our loving Heavenly Father will continue to love you and to work with you, and to show you every area that you need to yield to *Christ's love*. The Holy Spirit is willing to show you any adjustment that you need to make in your thinking and lifestyle.

You are not alone. God's grace, which is His *divine power working within you*, will heal your broken heart and fix everything that needs to be fixed. Stay humble, and the more of God's Word that you plant within, the more of a harvest you will reap. Soon you will have a visible harvest everyone can see that is your testimony.

3

The Neglected Field

I have seen many people that struggle under the weight and strain of what God has called them to do. There is nowhere in the Scripture that says, "Be ye burdened."

The Word says in 1 Peter 5:7, "Casting all of

your care upon him; for he careth for you."

"For My yoke is easy and My burden is light."
(Matthew 11:30 NASB)

Jesus is the strong ox that bears the burden in the heat of the day. *His yoke is easy and His burden is light.* If you are carrying a heavy load, you need to learn to cast your care onto the Lord Jesus Christ. There is nothing too heavy for Him to carry, and there is nothing too small or trivial that Jesus does not care about.

We have to get unbelief out of our hearts and always *keep it out.* I will go even further and say that *unbelief is a luxury that none of us can afford.* It will make your life miserable. It may even cause you to make some other people miserable so that they don't want to be around you.

A Field Turned Into a Forest

In beautiful New England where I come from, you can have the most beautiful farm with the most beautiful tilled land. If you just leave that land alone and do not cultivate it, strange things will happen to that ground.

Uncultivated land is soon hard and unusable ground. Just leave land alone and soon you have the weeds, then the grasses, then the bushes, and soon the little trees.

It only takes about five years for a beautiful field to be well on its way to being a forest. Soon the alders, spruce trees, poplar, and white birch come to grow and to stay.

How often I have heard older people say, "I

remember when this was all fields and now look at it." If that can happen to the soil of a crop-bearing field, what can happen to a man or woman's heart?

If you just start thinking about whatever pops into your head, and stop being fed the Word of Almighty God, it doesn't take long before the soil of your heart begins to get hard. Soon the thorns of Mark 4:7 that choke out the tender plants will appear.

You don't have to ever have this happen in your life. Every day and every year can bring an ever-increasing harvest of love, joy, peace, patience, kindness, goodness, faithfulness, gentleness, and self-control (Galatians 5:22-23).

It is never too late. The same Word that works for others will work for you and your family. For God is no respecter of persons

(Romans 2:11).

The Power of the Preached Word

"So then faith cometh by hearing and hearing by the Word of God." (Romans 10:17)

Instead of always trying to stop believing something that is wrong, there is another better way: Find a promise in Scripture and wrap your arms of faith around it.

Sit under the ministry of a mighty Holy Ghost preacher who is preaching the Word, and faith will come and stand by your seat. In fact, it will get on you and have you joyfully running up to the altar to receive the promise.

Sinners don't believe like they should, but when the Word is preached in power, something happens to them. That's how *divine healing* comes. *The Word is preached, and faith comes and says, "You don't have to die."*

That is also how the *Holy Ghost* comes with the evidence of speaking in other tongues as the Spirit gives the utterance. Someone gets fired up in *faith* as the *Word is preached.*

We would sure have a lot less problems in our churches if the Word was really preached. Strong churches have had the Word preached under the unction of the Holy Ghost for years.

"For after that in the wisdom of God the world by wisdom knew not God, it pleased God by the foolishness of preaching to save them that believe." (1 Corinthians 1:21)

It is so easy to believe something that is right when faith comes and a divine knowing just bubbles up in your spirit. Start believing something that is right today and then let God and grace build on that.

Determine that you are going to believe and do what is written in the Word.

4

The Boundary Lines of God's Word

I am a country boy that God sends to cities all around America to preach, win souls, lay hands on the sick, and see whole churches revived. But my roots are from the country, in the state of Maine.

I can tell you that country people care about where the boundary lines are on their farms and property. Not only do they care about it but they can point to it and usually show you a stake that is driven in the ground. Sometimes it is a fence or a stream or a tree, but they all know where the boundary is.

The boundary lines of that which we believe come from what is written in the Word of almighty God. What matters isn't what we feel or what old brother so-and-so had to say about a particular subject, unless what they believed was based on and backed up by the Word of God.

The day that you start letting what the Word says determine what you will believe and do is the day that you start being supernaturally blessed. The soil of someone's heart which is filled with doubt can never produce. But if you will allow the Holy

Spirit in prayer to plow the soil of your heart, it will change your life forever.

When God puts His finger on attitudes and unforgiveness in your life, it is for only one reason: so that He can set you up for increase. People that have plowed and have pure hearts are ready to have great increase in their lives.

Oh, how often has God's love and wisdom shown me where to change, and then supernaturally given me the grace to change. Then dramatic harvest and blessing would come into my life and family. God's love and goodness changed me forever when I couldn't change myself.

Good soil will always receive the seed of God's Word for a 100-fold return. God can change anyone and He always changes us for the better. And He most always starts with our heart.

The Humble Heart that Relies on God Alone

Have you ever noticed if you go to a doctor, the first thing that they look at is not your big toe? The physician's stethoscope is immediately put upon your heart so that the trained one can listen.

The next time that you bow at an altar by your bed or in God's house, the Holy Spirit will listen to your heart. Most likely to check and see that it has not grown cold and hard.

"The sacrifices of God are a broken spirit: a broken and a contrite heart, O God, thou wilt not despise." (Psalm 51:17)

How often, after traveling thousands of miles or preaching night after night, I have asked God to guard my heart. I never want to grow hard in my heart because of disappointment or become exalted and proud because of success.

By God's grace, I never want to have even a trace of an attitude that says I have learned how to minister by myself and in my own strength. Without Jesus and the flow of the Holy Spirit in our lives, we can do nothing eternal.

Anytime that I ever miss it and am not flowing in the Fruit of the Spirit like I should, I do something. I pray and ask the Lord to help me, and I lay my heart open before God and ask Him to change it. A heart that is pleasing to the Lord is always a heart that is overflowing with

God's love.

The anointing is not operating in the strength of fleshly charisma and human talent. If I ever sense that I am too important for a little crowd, or if I hear myself with pride discussing the large churches that we go to, I ask God to change my heart. Our successes and victories are only to be talked about in the context that they glorify the Lord or inspire the discouraged.

Without the Lord, we are nothing. Without Him, we can do nothing of eternal value. But with a pure heart relying on God, we can change the world. Hardness within brings spiritual famine and crop failure in your life.

The Heart We All Need

Have you ever noticed that children do not have hard hearts? I wish that I had been there that day when Jesus showed the crowd a little boy or a little girl.

"Except ye be converted, and become as little children, ye shall not enter into the kingdom of heaven." (Matthew 18:3)

Have you ever noticed how trusting a child is and how teachable they are? How they get upset with another child on the playground and then they *quickly* get over it? The tender heart of a child is so precious. The tender heart of a child is what we all need.

Hard-Hearted People Have a Hard Life

On another occasion, Jesus began to strongly correct the disciples. In Mark 16:14, what was the Lord dealing with them about? *Unbelief and the hardness of their hearts.*

"Afterward He appeared to the eleven themselves as they were reclining at the table; and He reproached them for their unbelief and hardness of heart, because they had not believed those who had seen Him after He had risen." (Mark 16:14 NASB)

Hard-hearted people can't receive the Word and also cannot stand upon the Word for as long as it takes. I like what Bro. Jerry Savelle teaches: "When you are willing to stand on the Word for as long as it takes, you won't have to stand for long."

Oh, the tremendous treasures in this life and in the world to come that some people—even some Christians—do not receive. They do not receive what they desire and even need at times, all because they do not receive and believe the Word.

You need to not only be saved from sin but to walk in the Blessing. It is hard for some to receive the Scriptures. Hard for them to believe. *Hard-hearted people have a hard life.*

The Holy Spirit will work within our lives and make us tender if we let Him. The work which the Spirit of God accomplishes is an inner work. A work of the Spirit. *The drawing power of the Holy Spirit is a supernatural work of God's grace.*

Do you sense something deep within speaking to you? It's a calling of God's grace to a higher level. Are you tired of just surviving? Weary in well doing? Barely keeping your head above water? God has called you to mighty things for God's glory. But the things of the Spirit have to be received by faith and acted upon in faith.

Receiving God's great love will do more for you in five minutes than twenty years of religion.

Don't try to fix yourself, straighten yourself out, redeem yourself, or impress God with your works. Just humbly come and ask God to forgive you. Say, "Jesus, I want your help." Peace will come. Supernatural strength will come.

5

Jesus the Restorer

"That he would grant you, according to the riches of his glory, to be strengthened with might by his Spirit in the inner man;

That Christ may dwell in your hearts by faith; that ye, being rooted and grounded in love, May be able to comprehend with all saints what is the breadth, and length, and depth, and height;

and to know the love of Christ, which passeth knowledge, that ye might be filled with all the fulness of God." (Ephesians 3:16-19)

When you begin to realize how much God loves you then your expectancy and hope will arise. We live in a world filled with *hope-less* people.

Do you feel hopeless about your future? Your finances? Your marriage? Let your inner man be filled with the love that God has for you. Jesus is a fixer. *A restorer.* And what Jesus restores is worth so much more than the original.

When your heart is right, God's Word can be planted there. When God's Word is planted in good soil, it *always* yields results. Then God will bring *supernatural increase* into your life. You will *reap and keep.*

The Goodness of Our Heavenly Father

How many of you have been praying that your kids will always struggle and constantly live in poverty? Have you been longing that they will always be poor? "Lord, let them always work in a dead-end job with no hope for advancement."

Are you praying for your children, "Lord, let them toil in discouragement, barely making ends meet"? If that is how you feel, then I would not want you for a parent.

No earthly parent wants their child to suffer in poverty. Something in a mother or father wants their child to prosper. It was put there by God. It reflects the heart of God. *God is a good God.*

Struggle Is of the devil

It's worth it to serve Jesus in this life and in the life to come. Let the seed of God's Word take deep root within your heart. Nurture that seed by being around other believers. I love everybody, but I am not close friends with anybody that perpetually is filled with doubt and unbelief.

Some precious people constantly, on a day by day basis, feed their spirit doubt and unbelief. Doubt is a pathway that can lead to a highway of unbelief. Ask God to weed out anything in your heart that shouldn't be there. *Have faith in God.*

Is it possible that God intended for Adam to continually expand the Garden of Eden as he tended it? Remember, after the Fall, something happened to the soil and Adam had to continually struggle by the sweat of his brow (Genesis 3:17-19).

There is no struggle like having the soil of your heart affected by doubt and unbelief. *Struggling is of the devil and people who believe God and walk in the spirit do not struggle.*

Your faith may be tested, but when you need more faith, just plant more of the Word in the good soil of your heart. *Then cultivate the faith that you already have by confessing the written and revealed promises of God.*

God has such great plans for your life and whole family, here and in the endless, joyful eternity.

"Their children will be successful everywhere; an entire generation of godly people will be blessed. They themselves will be wealthy, and their good deeds will last forever." (Psalm 112:2-3 NLT)

The garden of your life will expand. The soil of your life will be good ground. It will be soil ready to produce a mighty harvest when joined with the seed of *God's faithful Word* and faith. A harvest of 30 and 60 and 100-fold return.

The garden of your life will be a God-glorifying harvest in this life that the enemy can't steal and that lasts for all of time and eternity. That's what God does with *seed and soil.*

Pray this prayer to ask Jesus into your heart and be saved for all of eternity:

Heavenly Father, in Jesus' name, please forgive me for all of my sin. I believe that You are the true Son of God, and I claim Your shed blood on the cross of Calvary to pay for my sins. I believe that God raised Jesus from the dead. Wash me clean from all of my sins, and I will serve You the rest of my life. One day, I want to go to Heaven and live with You forever.

After you have prayed this prayer, contact me and I will send you material that will bless you and help you to grow on your Christian journey.

PO Box 24, Bangor, ME 04402

markdunfeeministries@gmail.com

markdunfee.com

Made in the USA
Columbia, SC
03 April 2021